Series / Number 02-023

The Efficacy of Threats in International Interaction Strategies

CHARLES LOCKHART

⑤ SAGE PUBLICATIONS / Beverly Hills / London

For information address:

SAGE PUBLICATIONS, INC.
275 South Beverly Drive
Beverly Hills, California 90212

SAGE PUBLICATIONS LTD
St George's House / 44 Hatton Garden
London EC1N 8ER

International Standard Book Number 0-8039-0361-x

Library of Congress Catalog Card No. L.C. 73-92217

FIRST PRINTING

When citing a professional paper, please use the proper form. Remember to cite the
correct Sage Professional Paper series title and include the paper number. One of the
two following formats can be adapted (depending on the style manual used):

(1) AZAR, E. E. (1972) "International Events Interaction Analysis." Sage Professional Papers in International Studies, 1, 02-001. Beverly Hills and London: Sage
Pubns.

OR

(2) Azar, Edward E. 1972. *International Events Interaction Analysis.* Sage Professional Papers in International Studies, vol. 1, series no. 02-001. Beverly Hills and
London: Sage Publications.

CONTENTS

The Efficacy of Threats in International Interaction Strategies

CHARLES LOCKHART

Few international theorists would deny the positive contributions threats provide for the resolution of international conflicts. Yet widespread recognition of the volatile and counterproductive impact threats often exert on conflicts among nations exists, as well. Threats cannot be implemented indiscriminately *and* effectively, and since the boundaries on the productive range of threat application remain murky, statecraft and science both demand a clearer understanding of these limitations. Toward this end, this essay offers a theoretical discussion of three general problem areas associated with the use of threats—and an intensive examination of an instance in diplomatic history (the Agadir crisis of 1911) which highlights these difficulties.

One factor limiting the efficacy of threats derives from a pervasive yet rarely acknowledged problem which attends international communications at large. Arguments challenging the accuracy of communications among states have penetrated the study of international politics only recently. Instances of communications failure are still commonly viewed as

AUTHOR'S NOTE: *Glenn H. Snyder, Paul Diesing, Robert Jervis, John P. Lovell, Terry Nardin and Charles Planck provided criticism and encouragement on earlier drafts of this essay. Research for this essay was supported in part by National Science Foundation Grant GS 3227.*

anomalies, and neither the memoirs of statesmen—nor the theories of prominent scholars generally—entail any concern with *misperception* as a systematic or even recurrent phenomenon. Yet considering the difficulties individuals with far greater common experience—as friends, lovers, families or co-workers—have communicating among themselves, accurate communication is a curious presupposition for international affairs. Recent work dealing with both adversary (Sigal, 1970) and ally (Neustadt, 1970) relationships in international politics indicates spokesmen for different states approach international issues from diverse perspectives formed by their parochial national experiences. Other increasingly influential efforts (such as White, 1966) argue that misperception pervades diplomatic experience. Statesmen of various nations are shown to live in different conceptual worlds linked only by the most tenuous communications bridges. These works picture misperception as the rule, not the exception, in diplomacy.

THREATS AND MISPERCEPTION PATTERNS

Specific aspects of this general communications malady relate to the use of threats. Actual incompatibility of goals among actors—two states claim the same piece of territory—is apt to lie at the heart of international struggles. But mutually exclusive objectives provide only the core for most conflicts among nations. Conflict also arises through misperception, and faulty communications often create a penumbra of phony issues around the core. Jervis (1968) has culled the literature of cognitive psychology and philosophy of science to suggest a misperception syndrome which may arise as disparate national perspectives clash. These perspectives distort the scope of conflict by multiplying the issues which the contending parties perceive as threatened.

These additional issues arise from erroneous images common to the perspectives of international adversaries. These images often enable "reasonable men" to swallow incredibly inaccurate interpretations of an adversary's activity. Fears implicit in the anarchical international system lead statesmen to focus their attention on phenomena which present possibilities of danger, and statesmen develop characteristic misperception patterns as a result of this selective attention. Through this "adversary syndrome," statemen tend to exaggerate both the aggressiveness and the coordinated planning—in short, the threatening nature—of opposing nations. Thus they usually carry grandiose perceptions of the opponent's goals, and the opponent's awkward signals are frequently mistaken for proof of aggressive intent. In addition, statesmen tend to define legitimacy in terms of their own experience; they fail to realize their actions are inconsistent with other conceptions of legitimacy and often appear threatening to others. The adversary then is held responsible for all aggressiveness and provocation. Since these misperceptions are reciprocal, the leaders of each national unit find themselves reluctantly taking measures to counter the monumental, unprovoked threats of other national units. Policy measures based on misperception of this nature are often counterproductive in that they are apt to needlessly exacerbate existing conflicts. Sino-American relations during the 1950s offer a particularly clear example of this problem. Policies rooted in misperception may even give rise to conflict spirals in instances in which no conflict of interest actually exists. The height of folly associated with policies arising from exaggerated perceptions of threats is that initially erroneous perceptions can develop into self-fulfilling prophecies. That is, a benign nation which is treated as an adversary for a period of time may well become hostile.

In addition to the problem of selective attention to international phenomena, statesmen display patterns of selective interpretation of the phenomena to which they are attentive; and conceptual difficulties concerning the nature of threats add to the problems arising from the adversary syndrome. Baldwin (1971) provides a commendable analysis of portions of this confusion. The everyday notion of a threat implies a *relationship* between parties: one party attempts to influence another's action through the contingent application of punishment, and the target party recognizes this attempt. But varying interests cause researchers and political actors to focus on specific aspects of this relationship. To some a threat is an *undertaking.* In this sense a threat is considered an influence attempt, and the target's perceptions are of little concern. For others threats are a target's *perceptions of anticipated harm,* and the identity or even the existence of an initiator is virtually ignored. Those who scrutinize undertakings and perceptions of harm respectively are simply dealing with different phenomena, and (as Baldwin points out) game theorists and social psychologists, among others, often talk past—rather than to—one another.

Anarchical conditions provide the link between these conceptual difficulties and the erroneous perception of threats. In Herz' (1951) terms the "security dilemma" resulting from international anarchy rivets attention to anticipated harm. From the perspective of any one national unit the specter of competitors limited only by their will and might indeed portends "a life solitary, poore, nasty, brutish and short." Although international conditions hardly amount to Hobbes' vision of units driven by fears for their security or by unquenchable desires for power foraying continually against one another, many nations face enough hostility and uncertainty to incur regular anticipation of harm. Against this alarming array of threats posed by the international environment, national leaders contrast their own limited undertakings aimed at threatening others. Threats then appear to be imposed by adversaries far more regularly than they flow from the nation. But this imbalance stems largely from a misleading comparison of two variations of threats: perceptions of harm, and undertakings designed to influence the action of others. Equivalency fails here since perceptions of harm often exist—particularly in anarchical milieux where unfounded fears abound—in the absence of a threat relationship entailing a target *and an initiator*. The Lebanese crisis of 1958 serves as a classic example of nations holding perceptions of harm in the absence of adversaries initiating threats. The Lebanese situation was an imaginary conflict of interest which the Soviet Union and the United States both perceived as threatening for a brief period (Stover, 1971).

The exaggeration of foreign threats is heightened through a dubious shorthand widely used by strategists to calculate threats in terms of anticipated harm. According to this algorithm anarchical conditions make reliance on conscious signals of an adversary's intentions a risky business. Indices such as actual capabilities furnish a safer basis for discerning threats. Discernible capabilities may be deceptive as well, and the "realist" may prefer to prepare for contingencies beyond his adversary's recognized range of response. While no succinct formulation of this principle can do justice to its most sophisticated advocates, this approach sanctions negatively biased images of an adversary's intentions and capabilities on the principle: better "safe" than sorry. It assumes that expecting and preparing for the severest possible contingencies provides the best defense of national interests. For advocates of this rule the dangers involved in creating imaginary diabolical fiends are less fearful than the possibility of being outflanked in a struggle for national survival. This preference exists in spite of the recognized tendency for excessive preparations to generate the very circumstances of escalated competition or conflict which they are designed to deter. Richardson's (Rapoport, 1957) study of arms races is a famous example of counterproductive preparations, and Khrushchev's frustrated cry that his deployment of strategic weapons in Cuba almost precipitated the threat it was designed to deter, a United States invasion, provides another instance (Current Digest of the Soviet Press, 1963).

Jervis (forthcoming) carefully examines how arms races and drives for colonial acquisition have fueled unnecessary and counterproductive conflict spirals. The realist argument which can result in needless conflict spirals often uses the adversary's capabilities as working hypotheses for judging his intentions. Reliance on this index is cited as necessary since intentions cannot be ascertained. If interpreted strictly this argument is nonsense. The very distinction between ally and adversary presumes that intentions can be effectively judged to some degree. The capabilities of the ally are grudgingly accepted since their intended use directs them against the adversary. Deriving an adversary's intentions from his capabilities errs by dichotomizing in an instance in which shades and variations are requisite. The terms ally and adversary denote broad tails of a continuous distribution, not a discrete, dichotomous variable.[1] Statesmen usually have no difficulty protecting their interests by recognizing the limits of collective goods shared with allies; rarely indeed does a state support an ally in defense of interests providing no common benefit. But statesmen often fail to recognize limits on the conflicting interests threatened by adversaries. Recognition of these limits is crucial to the efficacy of threats, for if targets regularly misperceive threats through exaggeration, target compliance is apt to suffer.

VARIATIONS IN THE IMPACT OF THREATS

In international affairs threats are simply volatile signals. The international system allows all member states the delusion of nominal equality. Often, through parity of their own resources or through alliances, international antagonists hold a rough equality. But through a threat one party arrogates to himself the right to demand another to act in a certain way. This act necessarily challenges accepted rules of conduct among equals, and threats have at least two independent counterproductive aspects. One aspect is that threats engage additional issues or values for the target, and this makes cooperation more costly for him. This consideration resembles the supergame of experimental game theory—albeit in degenerate form (Snyder, 1971: 94-102). If a target submits to threats in one instance the initiator's appetite for easy gains may only be whetted. Targets are then reluctant to submit to threats in any given instance due to the precedent this might set for future, and perhaps increasingly frequent, encounters. Several of President Kennedy's advisors in the Cuban crisis were reluctant to accept Soviet strategic missiles in Cuba primarily because they felt acceptance would lead directly to new Soviet challenges elsewhere in Latin America and in West Berlin. This is only one instance of the "Munich complex" (Barnet, 1968) exhibited by many Western statesmen whose formative diplomatic experience came in dealings with the Third Reich.

A second counterproductive aspect of threats stems from their tendency to shift the perspectives under which conflict is waged from the sphere of strategic interaction (games) to the sphere of fights (Rapoport, 1960). In other words the specter of manipulation may so irritate the target that he abandons a rational or strategic approach to interaction and strikes out blindly at his adversary with little thought for the mutual disaster entailed in escalated conflict. While threats rarely so enrage an entire national decision unit, individual decision makers do often lose a strategic perspective. The reaction of some United States military leaders to the destruction of a U-2 reconnaissance plane late in the Cuban crisis illustrates the loss of strategic perspective. Also the initial or "gut" reaction of a decision unit to a threat is often a brief rage which suspends strategic action momentarily.

In spite of these generally negative associations threats do vary in their impact on targets. One factor involved in this variation is the threat vulnerability of the target. Threat vulnerability indicates the relative ease with which a party can be coerced into submission through threats. Operationalization of this concept entails ordinally ranking each party's preferences and comparing one party's preference structure with the preferences of his adversary. A rough index can be constructed by relating the basic structure of particular international conflicts in terms of the payoffs for general accommodative and coercive approaches to the configuration of rewards and punishments found in symmetrical two-by-two games. Three such games—Bully, Prisoner's Dilemma and Chicken—are shown in Figure 1.

Although each party in the Bully game would prefer to have its opponent back down than to face mutual coercion (war), both prefer war to a compromise solution. So there is virtually no vulnerability to threats in this game, and threats merely precipitate an inevitable war. Japanese-American relations prior to World War II illustrate this condition. Chicken exhibits the greatest threat vulnerability of the symmetrical configurations shown in Figure 1. Here each party prefers having his own cooperation exploited by the adversary to receiving the payoff for mutual stubbornness. Chicken thus offers a productive setting for mutual threats and, as Schelling (1960 and 1966) has shown, is essentially a race for preemptive commitment. The Berlin crisis of 1948-1949 approximates this condition. Prisoner's Dilemma stands between the Bully and Chicken models in terms of threat vulnerability. Here threats are tricky since each party prefers war to exploited cooperation. But each prefers compromise to war, so careful application of threats holds some promise. The Agadir crisis of 1911 is a rough example of this type of conflict, and the impact

BULLY

		Column	
		Accommodation	Coercion
Row	Accommodation	2, 2	1, 4
	Coercion	4, 1	3, 3

PRISONER'S DILEMMA

		Column	
		Accommodation	Coercion
Row	Accommodation	3, 3	1, 4
	Coercion	4, 1	2, 2

CHICKEN

		Column	
		Accommodation	Coercion
Row	Accommodation	3, 3	2, 4
	Coercion	4, 2	1, 1

Figure 1: **SYMMETRICAL GAMES REPRESENTING VARIOUS LEVELS OF THREAT VULNERABILITY** (numbers are ordinal)

of threats in this medium vulnerability crisis will be examined in some detail below.

Some international conflicts are better represented by asymmetrical combinations of these and other payoff structures. Figure 2 provides some asymmetrical examples with important empirical referents in diplomatic history. Column (Chicken) in the asymmetrical Bully-Chicken conflict has the greatest threat vulnerability of any of the parties shown in Figures 1 and 2. Not only is war his least acceptable alternative, but he faces an opponent who prefers this alternative to mutual compromise. So Row, the bully in this game, can freely threaten Column and expect productive results. Row, on the other hand, is impervious to threats from Column. This situation is unusual in international conflict, but the Anglo-French Fashoda crisis of 1898 and the rump Czechoslovakia crisis of 1939 approximate these conditions. In these instances the British and the Germans were able to bully the French and the Czechs respectively into the lower, left-hand outcome of exploited cooperation. The Prisoner's

BULLY-CHICKEN

		Column	
		Accommodation	Coercion
Row	Accommodation	2, 3	1, 4
	Coercion	4, 2	3, 1

PRISONER'S DILEMMA-CHICKEN

		Column	
		Accommodation	Coercion
Row	Accommodation	3, 3	1, 4
	Coercion	4, 2	2, 1

MISPERCEPTION (Prisoner's Dilemma-Chicken)

		Column	
		Accommodation	Coercion
Row	Accommodation	3, 3	1, 4
	Coercion	4, 2	2, 1

Figure 2: ASYMMETRICAL GAMES REPRESENTING VARIOUS LEVELS OF THREAT VULNERABILITY (numbers are ordinal)

Dilemma-Chicken schema offers disproportionate advantage to the party with Prisoner's Dilemma preferences (Row) who in contrast to Chicken (Column) prefers war to withdrawal in the absence of mutual cooperation. The bargaining stages of the Cuban missile crisis approximate these conditions for the United States and the Soviet Union respectively. Had the escalation reached beyond the violence threshhold, however, the crisis might well have been transformed to an example of symmetrical Prisoner's Dilemma.

Prisoner's Dilemma-Chicken also captures important aspects of the common misperception syndrome discussed in the previous section. Row in the misperception version of Prisoner's Dilemma-Chicken in Figure 2 recognizes threats alone will not induce him to back down. His preferences are arranged in Prisoner's Dilemma fashion, and he prefers war to backing down unilaterally. But Row perceives Column to face a Chicken structure, and Row then thinks of Column as being highly vulnerable to threats. If the issues at stake are more important to Column than Row realizes, Column may have a Prisoner's Dilemma preference structure, and Row's attempts to wring concessions from him are apt to lead to war. Row's problem (of ascertaining Column's actual preferences) is often complicated, since Column may have an interest in misrepresenting his preferences. If Column has Chicken preferences but a gambling nature, misrepresenting his preference structure as Prisoner's Dilemma may enable him to gain mutual accommodation rather than having to settle for exploited cooperation.

Another factor contributing to variation in the impact of threats is the particularly counterproductive impact associated with certain threats. Snyder (1969) distinguishes between threats which have only communicative value and those which carry committal value as well. The former, warnings, simply communicate a preexisting commitment or minimally acceptable state of affairs to an adversary. A statesman uses a warning to inform an adversary state that its actions violate his own minimal tolerance boundaries, and a warning conveys the message that, unless the adversary alters his actions, responses which will counter their impact on the statesman's own values will be forthcoming. These threats appeal to empathy and reciprocity as they warn of the mutually undesirable consequences of the adversary pressing intolerable conditions on his target. In addition warnings mark off the limits of the initiator's immediate aspirations rather than confronting the target with open-ended demands. United States efforts to gain the removal of Soviet strategic weapons from Cuba have generally been interpreted as classic warnings. While the target of such threats certainly perceives and is irritated by the manipulative aspect they carry, the impact of manipulation is muted by recognition of the warner's central endeavours to save both parties from an impending common disaster and to clarify his essential goals.

Threats of the committal variety serve a communicative function, but they also provide a requisite contribution to a budding commitment. The purpose of these threats is not to warn an adversary he has violated a tolerance boundary but to create a new—and often, to the adversary, a seemingly unnecessary—commitment to a condition in excess of the previous minimally acceptable state of affairs. These are the threats Schelling (1960 and 1966) has analyzed so thoroughly in an effort to understand how signals function in the construction of commitments. Western perceptions of Khrushchev's ultimata in the 1958-1962 Berlin situation provide recent, unproductive examples of threats in this category. No notion of empathy or reciprocity mitigates the manipulation of these threats, which exemplify an essence of brinkmanship. The target of such threats recognizes his adversary is taking needless selfish advantage of the common interest in avoiding disaster by pressing the target dangerously far out on the slippery slope bordering the brink of disaster. Committal threats give the target the impression that the initiator is asking for more than he really needs. They exacerbate the problem of issue or value engagement since the initiator appears to be on a fishing expedition asking, not for what he needs, but for whatever the target will concede. Confronting a target with the realization that he is being pushed around at the whim of his adversary can actually destroy the threat vulnerability of the target by enlarging the long-term or supergame costs of compliance.

Committal threats also frequently include highly visible coercive tactics that give rise to incentives which reinforce the target's supergame considerations for resisting manipulation. Brusk coercive tactics shatter hopes for empathy and reciprocity and create anger by leaving the impression that the threat initiator values the target's humiliation as well as the concrete issues at stake. Thus committal threats are particularly irritating, not only because of what they demand, but because of the insulting manner in which the demands are couched. And the perception of receiving calculated humiliation can quickly drive a target from a strategic mode of action into a fight.[2]

Additional problems of threat implementation arise from interaction between misperception and factors contributing to variation in threat impact—threat vulnerability and the warning-committal threat distinction. Statesmen recognize the national units they represent will fight before giving up crucial values at stake in particular conflicts—that is, their decision units face Prisoner's Dilemma preferences on some issues. However, statesmen often misperceive the adversary's predicament as Chicken and thereby exaggerate his threat vulnerability. The misperception syndrome discussed in the previous section helps to explain this mistake. The statesman's own nation is viewed as sustaining only legitimate defensive endeavours. But adversary states are engaged in continual aggressive forays. The challenges of adversary states do not represent the defense of crucial values, but rather are probes of the statesman's own resolve. These challenges can be rebuffed without fear of retaliation since adversary states can withdraw their probes in the face of firmness without violating their crucial tolerances. Visions such as these are common misperceptions. The Chinese intervention in Korea as United States forces approached the Yalu River punctured one such misperception bubble for the United States. And an adversary perceived to face a Chicken payoff structure may actually be defending essential goals for which he is willing to fight.

National decision units, particularly adversary units, also communicate poorly among one another, and target nations often perceive committal threats when a nation has sent a warning. The target then treats the desperate signal of the initiator as aggressive coercion. This mistake is serious enough, but further repercussions are apt to follow. The party which suffers a target's ridiculing of its earnest warning as an insidious manipulative ploy will probably not be capable of viewing signals from this target as conscientious attempts to warn of impending danger, and the original conflict of interest may easily become lost in a spiral of escalating recriminations flowing from false conceptions of one another's signals. The escalation of conflict in Northern Ireland from a civil rights protest in 1969 to an independence struggle by 1971 bears elements of this interaction between misperception and the impact of particular types of threats.

THREATS AND A TARGET'S DOMESTIC SITUATION

Constraints provided by the domestic polity served by the national leaders of a target state also limit the efficacy of threats. Halperin and Kanter (1973) have recently turned their attention toward a similar consideration. They point out that the national leaders of most modern states arise from and are most concerned with the problems of their domestic domains. Their interests, experience and expertise—not to mention their constituencies and thus their futures—belong primarily to the realm of domestic activity. Attention turns toward foreign affairs only as some aspect of the international environment appears to threaten domestic interests. Although this may happen regularly, the intrusions of the international environment force national politicians to deal with intricate matters foreign to the focus of their interests. Inexperience and parochial outlook mark the national politician's ventures in the international arena. Thus, his international actions are rarely characterized by the knowledgeable, adroit handling with which the accomplished national leader soothes the wounds of his convulsed domestic polity. United States foreign policy in Southeast Asia over the last three decades tragically demonstrates such inexperience and parochialism.

The importance of this domestic orientation for the impact of threats stems in part from the hard-line attitudes toward foreign threats common to many domestic factions. Powerful domestic interests are frequently unenlightened—if not chauvinistic—with respect to the problems of foreign counterparts. And the national leader faced with a disparity between the well-known, hard-line demands of his own polity and the unfamiliar threats of foreign powers may well adhere closely to the constraints of the domestic groups and (while hoping for the best) let the chips fall where they may in terms of international consequences.[3] As an example of this tendency, Allison and Halperin (1972) contrast McNamara's argument that the international costs of the Soviet deployment of strategic weapons in Cuba were inconsequential particularly in comparison to the risks involved in gaining their removal (Hilsman, 1964: 195) against the concern of President Kennedy and several of his advisors that ignoring the strategic installations—particularly in light of the Cuban fiasco in Kennedy's recent past—would have dire domestic consequences leading perhaps to impeachment (Kennedy, 1969: 67).

Neustadt (1970) offers another problem arising from the domestic orientation of many national leaders. Familiarity with the operations of their own governments often leads national leaders to exert influence on what they feel to be counterpart forms (roles or institutions) of other nations forgetting that function does not always follow form. During the Fashoda crisis of 1898, for example, the British applied pressure to Delacassé, (the French foreign minister), but they missed the parochial ministry of colonies bureaucrats who were pressing the Fashoda affair (Brown, 1970: 136-140). Had the British clearly noticed the difference in preferences between Delcassé and the bureaucracy, they might still have missed the relative independence French bureaucrats enjoyed with respect to short-lived ministers—since this independence constrasted starkly with disciplined British practices. Delcassé's dire need to represent hard-line French public opinion in spite of his own preference for improved Anglo-French relations would also have appeared strange and perhaps contrived to perceptions based on the more consensual and stable British experience (Brown, 1970: 126-131).

As Delcassé's Fashoda experience testifies, the domestic polity plagues even the most sophisticated statesman who is minimally hampered by inexperience and parochial outlook. Such statesmen rarely occupy positions enabling them to put this sophistication to unencumbered use. They are invariably dependent on significant segments of their domestic polities for support. Inasmuch as they well realize parochial, chauvinistic nationalist forces are capable of dealing severely with statesmen who treat the dangers of foreign adversaries too lightly for their tastes, sophisticated statesmen are often reluctant (if not unable) to respond to international conflicts with the restraint their judgment suggests. Understanding the multifarious aspects of international affairs is often separated from the influence necessary to direct action. The lingering grip of McCarthyism on United States policy toward China and Southeast Asia illustrates the magnitude of the difficulties which statesmen have to overcome (Ellsberg, 1972).

The early attacks on Acheson and Truman for the "loss" of China also demonstrates the statesman's dependence on viable relations with his domestic polity. But this example illustrates a different aspect of the statesman's relationship with his constituency. Statesmen often rely on hard-line domestic attitudes, and may even attempt to develop such attitudes, in order to bolster the resistance they can offer to foreign pressures. As a threat target, the statesman who wishes to present an intransigent position to a threat initiator certainly strengthens his case if he can demonstrate that any sign of reconciliation on his part would only lead to his dismissal by other and more hard-nosed domestic leaders. In the autumn of 1949 events in China caught up with Acheson and Truman, and they were simply trapped by the cold war attitudes they had struggled to intensify two years earlier in order to win domestic support for the Truman Doctrine and the Marshall Plan.

THREATS IN THE AGADIR CRISIS OF 1911

The factors suggested above to limit the efficacy of threats—misperception patterns, variations in threat impact and parochial domestic attitudes—merit more thorough examination than that furnished by the cursory examples which have illustrated the argument so far. Threats which exist only as figments in the imagination of apprehensive statesmen, which by their nature necessarily contribute more to conflict escalation than to conflict resolution, or through which a statesman is overpowered by chauvinistic elements of his own polity, are not apt to be productive; and a lengthy scrutiny of a series of related counterproductive instances will clarify limitations on the efficacy of threats. International crises provide a lucrative medium for examining the impact of threats on the management and resolution of conflict issues among states. Crisis issues tend to be concrete and urgent. These attributes focus issues clearly, so the bare bones of conflict are more starkly outlined than during tranquil background periods. Against these focused issues the impact of threats may be clearly traced, and insight into the interaction of threats and conflicts of interest can be derived. Naturally, the insight of any single crisis will be biased and incomplete from the standpoint of generalization.

The choice of the Agadir crisis deserves explanation. The lack of familiarity which this crisis evokes is offset by several factors. First, the crisis lies far enough back in history to be noncontroversial and of little partisan concern. Since scholars as well as statesmen hold biased perspectives, this is an important factor. Second, the crisis may be examined in terms of memoirs and historical scholarship from the perspectives of all major participants, and this represents a distinct advantage over most recent crises. Also, the memoirs and scholarship of the period may be checked against relevant public archival material. Third, the Agadir crisis is one in a series of interrelated crises among the European powers, and its close relationship with other crises provides insight into the interaction of threats and conflicts of interest over time. Fourth, the Agadir crisis offers an example of the middle ground of threat vulnerability—Prisoner's Dilemma—where threats are most dangerous. Although as an example of this middle range of threat vulnerability the Agadir crisis creates difficulties in terms of generalization to other categories of threat vulnerability, selection of this crisis does enable the analysis to focus on the situation where the limits on the productive range of threat application are most important, and the choice of this crisis is justified in part by the particularly clear limitations on the efficacy of threats it displays.

BACKGROUND TO THE CRISIS

The Agadir crisis pitted France and Britain against Germany and appeared superficially to be a struggle over control of Morocco.[4] Certainly the French were intrigued by the tottering Moroccan sultanate which was nominally independent although thoroughly penetrated by European influence, but France was the only party to the crisis for which the control of Morocco formed the central issue. French colonial interests felt their northwest African empire incomplete and, more importantly, insecure without the final increment of Morocco. The Moroccan side of the vague and rugged frontier with Algeria furnished a profitable base of operations for bandits, and if the French allowed this territory to fall into the hands of another European power, they could anticipate marauders directing even more sinister attacks against the French sphere of influence. Control of Morocco by the Germans, whom many French leaders felt existed only to wantonly intervene and wreak havoc on legitimate French interests, was a particularly threatening possibility. In Africa, as on the continent, the French perceived themselves to be containing German expansion.

For the Germans the Moroccan question involved broader issues of European diplomacy, however, and from their perspective a completely different crisis emerges. Although German businesses had concrete interests in Morocco, the German government's interest was primarily symbolic. Germany had not participated in the earlier colonial competition among the seafaring states of Western Europe. When Germany finally joined the fray there was little unclaimed territory left from which to build an empire. As one of the few remaining opportunities for colonial development, Morocco acquired special significance. If the future status of Morocco were decided without consideration for German interests—and consideration in this precedent setting instance might include compensation elsewhere, the German foreign office felt a severe blow would be dealt Germany's future voice in the councils of Europe and thus its strategic position. The Wilhelmstrasse sought to defend Germany from callous French efforts to affront legitimate German concerns in this manner (Bethmann-Hollweg, 1919: 29-31). More generally, German leaders held a lingering concern with what they perceived as the encirclement of Germany by hostile neighboring nations. The Anglo-French entente was an important aspect of this encirclement, and at times the Germans demonstrated an active interest in smashing the entente by pressuring the French to surrender important interests while the British watched idly from the sidelines. The 1905-1906 Franco-German crisis over Morocco is an example of this policy (Sontag, 1933: 94-95). Through such pressures the Germans hoped to gain French recognition of Britain's impotence on the continent and a virile Franco-German alliance which would shatter the encirclement of Germany. By 1911 several years of French intransigence toward improved relations with Germany—sparked primarily by German occupation of Alsace-Lorraine—and hopes among some German statesmen for improved relations with Britain muted this aspect of German Moroccan policy.

Still different interests lay behind British perceptions of the Moroccan question, and British incentives were less direct than the French yet more concrete than the German. The British government had no interest in acquiring Morocco, but the British recognized the sultan's weakness. And when the sultan's lamentable but inevitable demise occurred, the British wanted Morocco transferred to friendly, and preferably weak, hands since control of Morocco by a hostile power could close the western exit of the Mediterranean to the British navy. This would hamper communications with, and endanger the security of, Britain's vast colonial empire. So the British viewed a French Morocco more favorably than a German one, and they were even more pleased with the idea of a Spanish sphere of influence along the Mediterranean coast. But beyond this consideration Britain's presence in a Moroccan crisis in 1911 is attributable primarily to its alliance with France, the Entente Cordiale, and growing British preoccupation with the continental rather than the imperial arena. The entente, so the British thought, separated them from a confrontation with a German-led continental league. Britain's interests lay in ensuring French satisfaction with the entente. If Britain adequately supported France in its conflicts with Germany, such a league would be forestalled (Lowe and Dockrill, 1972: 40).

The crisis culminated a decade of French diplomacy aimed at securing Morocco. Beginning in 1901, Delcassé (then French foreign minister) worked out an intricate series of deals with the Italians, British and Spanish for the eventual French possession of Morocco (Andrew, 1968). Germany was noticeably omitted from these negotiations. During Delcassé's discussions with other states Germany indicated an interest in the Sous valley of southern Morocco, but the French perceived no legitimate German claims in this area and ignored these signals. The Germans were particularly upset by the arbitrary nature of the French position. If the French could manage to pay the British, the weak Italians and the inconsequential Spanish, they obviously could compensate a great power such as Germany. For the Germans the French refusal represented an attempt to single them out for humiliation. After several years of patient waiting the Germans eventually reacted with the kaiser's visit to the Moroccan sultan in Tangier in 1905. This protest of Germany's treatment precipitated the first Moroccan or Algeciras crisis.

The international conference held at Algeciras allowed the Germans an input on the Moroccan question and an opportunity to drive a wedge between Britain and France, but they were disappointed with the results as increased French—and to a lesser degree Spanish—influence over the nominally sovereign sultanate was accepted by the delegates, who appeared virtually united in their opposition to German interests (Anderson, 1930). This international decision resolved very little. The Germans continued to view the exclusively French penetration of Morocco as a threat to Germany's strategic position. In fact they were even more concerned after France's policy was sustained by the other European states at Algeciras. The French in turn regarded apprehensively the continuing German efforts to barge into the Moroccan question which, so the French felt, admitted no legitimate German interest. The French felt the Germans were not content with French humiliation arising from the occupation of Alsace-Lorraine; instead they were viciously challenging the French sphere of influence in Africa as well. Each state raised the other's hackles repeatedly through minor conflicts for the next few years. This intermittent conflict bothered both parties, however, and the two successfully negotiated an accord in 1909. Germany, through this agreement, promised to abandon political ambitions in Morocco in return for French recognition of German economic equality. Implementation of the agreement foundered on several obstacles. The fundamental difficulty involved the nature of the economic privileges the Germans desired. The *economic* concessions in which the Germans were most interested—mines, public works such as harbors and railways, and to a lesser extent loans—were considered by the French to be tools they needed for obtaining *political* control over Morocco.

Against this background of suspicion, fear and hostility a civil war developed in Morocco early in 1911. This chaos provided the pretext France needed to establish a protectorate over Morocco. A sizeable community of Europeans was isolated at the inland capital of Fez. There was general concern in European capitals—Berlin excepted—for the welfare of this community, and the Algeciras conference, which had legitimized French influence in this area, supported the French claim of responsibility for the safety of the community. Although the French claimed their expeditionary force would leave when order was restored, other European governments, particularly the German, realized the sultan's position had been so eroded by domestic incompetence and foreign penetration that a French protectorate was inevitable. The Germans had no wish to oppose the inevitable; they did demand compensation for French gains. The French had paid the Italians, the British and the Spanish for Morocco, and the Germans felt they were only demanding equal treatment. The Wilhelmstrasse thought the outcome of German claims would set a precedent for Germany's position as a European power. Failure to obtain compensation meant virtual exclusion from the council of nations which decided European issues. From the French viewpoint Europe had agreed at Algeciras in 1906 that France was to be predominant throughout most of Morocco. But the Germans had not accepted this European decision, and it had been necessary for the French to conclude a special agreement with them three years later in the accord of 1909. Yet the Germans still continued their provocation (Poincaré, 1922: 77-78, 91-92).

By 1911 the Germans and the French had frustrated each other's ambitions over the Moroccan question for a decade. Each side felt its own policy was a reasonable and legitimate defensive endeavor. The Germans perceived themselves as struggling to defend their voice in European decisions. In terms of taking the offensive German Agadir policy, at best, represented for some in the Wilhelmstrasse a halfhearted "try and see" attempt at cracking the entente. The French (and indirectly the British) felt they were containing a dangerous power. Each party perceived the difficulties as stemming from the unnecessarily provocative actions of the other. The Germans imagined conspiracies designed to cheat Germany of its legitimate European position. Entente statesmen held mental images of aggressive German challenges. Each side was deeply suspicious as to what ultimate goals prompted the other to such action, and although each felt threatened, neither was conscious of threatening the other. As Barlow (1940: 145) writes: "This mutual suspicion . . . translated every move of the opposing party into an act of chicanery or trickery; and this in the eyes of the victim justified acts of reprisal." Long years of conflict over the Moroccan question contributed to the misperception of the statesmen dealing with the 1911 episode. When thinking of the Moroccan question these statesmen recalled selectively the threats of the past and perceived the 1911 conflict in terms of important issues historically associated with the Moroccan question rather than in terms of the limited interests actually threatened by the intentions of the parties to the Agadir crisis.

THE FRENCH MOROCCAN COUP

In this hostile atmosphere the French started their expeditionary force toward the beleagured city of Fez. Although the French had considerable support throughout Europe for this move, even their British allies recognized the limited French predominance sanctioned at Algeciras was shattered. The power and authority of the sultan and his indigenous competitors was quite limited, and if Morocco was to be properly exploited by European business the French would have to assume responsibility for law and order. The Germans were particularly aware of this development. Their suggestion throughout the spring was German acquiescence to a French protectorate over Morocco in return for German compensation, but the French were not listening. Morocco lay virtually in their hands. The French force landed near Casablanca, moved along the coast to Rabat and finally headed inland on April 28, 1911.

On May 3, Kiderlen-Waechter (the German foreign minister) voiced his thoughts in a foreign office memorandum (Lepsius et al., 1925: 101-108). According to Kiderlen the basis for the Algeciras agreement, the sovereignty of Morocco, was now destroyed. Morocco stood on French bayonets and was a French protectorate in reality if not yet in name. This change released Germany from further respecting the Algeciras agreement. Nothing would be accomplished by opposing the French coup in Morocco, but Kiderlen thought the Germans could procure compensation commensurate with French gains. With the demise of the Algeciras agreement any European state was free to protect its nationals in Morocco. Germany could send ships to southern Moroccan harbors of Mogador and Agadir to protect German interests in this region. This activity would be distant enough from the Mediterranean to cause the British no concern, and the Germans could leisurely persist in holding these ports until the French offered compensation adequate to placate aggrieved German feelings.

The Germans made no immediate effort to counter what was for them the threat of a unilateral French settlement of the Moroccan question. They wished to allow the French enough rope to hang on promises of an early withdrawal before making their move. But Kiderlen's position was bolstered in early June (after the Spanish had landed forces along the Mediterranean coast of Morocco) by a memorandum from Zimmerman, a Wilhelmstrasse undersecretary (Lepsius et al., 1925: 142-149). Zimmermann felt the French were concerned about the German reaction and had discussed compensation unofficially—through Caillaux (then finance minister but subsequently premier), it was difficult to imagine the French would spontaneously offer Germany compensation. Germany should acquire security in southern Morocco which would ensure compensation. Zimmermann supported Kiderlen's idea of sending ships and thought Britain would remain aloof from these developments if it became known that the Germans were interested in compensation far to the south in the French Congo.

Conflicting national perspectives continued then to mold the French and German thoughts on the Moroccan question. The most naively parochial among the French leaders—the Foreign Minister Cruppi, for example—felt their nation was providing a humanitarian service of international (European) significance. The more cynical French leaders— such as Poincaré—recognized they were taking advantage of the current situation to complete the goal of a decade's diplomacy—French control of Morocco. All French leaders agreed that Germany's intervention in the Moroccan question was unwarranted and ominous in what it portended for future German goals. For the French the Agadir crisis was created by their apprehension over the threat of German expansion. In contrast to the 1905-1906 period, the German leadership in 1911 was not united in viewing the Moroccan question as crucial to Germany or as a lucrative forum for splitting the Entente Cordiale. Kaiser Wilhelm II and Chancellor Bethmann-Hollweg were both hoping for improved relations with Britain and grew increasingly disturbed as the crisis developed. Even Kiderlen focused on substantial French compensations rather than on attacking the entente. But the issue on which Kiderlen focused was important to the Wilhelmstrasse, and these men felt desperate. France was on the verge of securing Morocco without granting Germany the same courtesy as Italy, Britain and Spain. The threat Kiderlen, Zimmermann and Langwerth von Simmern visualized in this accomplishment was grave in terms of the precedent it set. They perceived in the French Agadir policy the exclusion of Germany from European decisions and the ensuing strengthened isolation of Germany. France had to be blocked from delivering such a blow, and the hostage port notion seemed the best bet.

THE KISSINGEN INTERLUDE

While the Germans adopted a policy of watchful waiting, the French were having second thoughts about winning German acquiescence. For although there was broad support for the French military expedition under existing circumstances, there was equally broad recognition that these circumstances were different than those of Algeciras. Even Grey, the British foreign secretary, allowed compensation was owed the Germans in view of recent French gains. The French began to view compensation as the most direct, if not the most pleasant, means of gaining requisite approval of their new Moroccan position. The French had what they wanted, and the were willing to conciliate Germany in some limited fashion. The French ambassador to Berlin, Jules Cambon, was directed to approach the Germans on the compensation issue.

Cambon's approach was cautious as the French were frightened by the demands of many German industrial groups for partition of Morocco, with the southern Sous valley going to Germany. To share their Moroccan prize with the aggressor holding Alsace-Lorraine was totally unacceptable. There had been some talk of compensation in the French Congo, and this might be acceptable, the French were hoping to avoid territorial compensation altogether by granting the Germans economic concessions in a variety of colonial areas. Cambon's feelers led him to Kiderlen who was vacationing at the baths of Kissingen. Cambon and Kiderlen met in Kissingen for discussions from June 20th to 22nd. After considerable diplomatic fencing, they made some progress. Cambon stated that no part of Morocco would be suitable for compensation but that the Germans might have luck elsewhere if France were granted a free hand in Morocan affairs. Kiderlen seemed amenable but, although each man tried to draw compensation suggestions from the other, the sessions ended without a discussion of particular compensation possibilities. [5]

Had these two diplomats effectively communicated their superiors' intentions during the Kissingen talks, there would have been no crisis in 1911. For at this juncture there were no important interests in conflict. The French wanted Morocco and virtually had it. They needed German acceptance of this development; German acceptance hinged on compensation, and the French were willing to comply. But unfortunately Cambon left Kissingen to consult with his superiors in Paris with Kiderlen imploring him to bring an offer on his return to Berlin. When Cambon reported at the Quai d'Orsay on the morning of June 24, however, he learned that the Monis government had fallen the previous evening. There was no foreign minister until June 29th when Caillaux, the new premier, prevailed on de

Selves to accept the post. Cambon did not return to Germany until early July, but his return was of little importance to Kiderlen who, discouraged by Cambon's reticence to offer specific proposals, decided to implement the German plan.

THE "PANTHER" EPISODE

During the late spring of 1911 the German government had swallowed dreams for a partition of Morocco and had accepted French predominance in Morocco contingent only on compensation. But the French had shown little empathy for their plight for several months, and the men in the Wilhelmstrasse felt their backs were to the wall. Now after the discussions at Kissingen their positions were reversed. The French had of necessity begun to explore the possibility of trading values with the Germans. And now the Germans failed to respond or even recognize French appeals for reconciliation. The discussions with Cambon at Kissingen did not leave Kiderlen with the impression that French compensation offers were imminent, and he moved quickly to secure final clearance of his May 3rd plan from the kaiser. The orders were set in motion before France had a new foreign minister. On July 1st a German gunboat, the "Panther," anchored in the fine natural harbor at Agadir.[6] The "Panther" had achieved notoriety as a provocateur in previous episodes of gunboat diplomacy (Vagts, 1956: 236), and when Schoen and Metternich (the German ambassadors to Paris and London respectively) announced its presence at Agadir, they created quite a stir.

The use of the "Panther" was carefully calculated by the Wilhelmstrasse. Thus Wolff's (1936: 4) remark that it has, "to be admitted that our people made long preparation for their mistakes and went about their frivolous moves without any precipitation," shows keen insight.[7] In part the Wilhelmstrasse deemed the move a necessary measure for assuring compensation since reliance on French goodwill was felt to be an insufficient safeguard for German interests. The Germans had too much experience with what they viewed as French bad faith to trust German compensation to French beneficence. A hostage port would ensure French good behavior on this score. But the German foreign office also thought the "Panther" would actually facilitate compensation for the French. German thinking, particularly that of Zimmermann and Langwerth von Simmern, ran that French public opinion would make a spontaneous offer of compensation to the German enemy difficult for any French government. The burden would be eased, however, if the necessity for offering compensation could be demonstrated (Pick, 1937: 326-328). This argument would be ludicrous if it were not so common and tragedy laden.

Additionally, German resort to the "Panther" may have arisen from, and provide an indicator of, differences of opinion within the German leadership. The kaiser had recently returned from a pleasant visit in Britain. He was not interested at this time in precipitating a conflict with the Entente Cordiale—particularly with Britain—and was in any case dubious by 1911 that the Moroccan question offered lucrative opportunities which merited undertaking the risks entailed in trying to smash the entente (Barlow, 1940: 226). Kiderlen may have desired to test the entente by putting pressure on France, but Kiderlen was, to his mind, careful to avoid putting pressure directly on Britain and indeed proclaimed a desire for improved relations with Britain. Lingering within the Wilhelmstrasse, however, was a preoccupation with Germany's encirclement. Some advisors may have grasped the Moroccan question and the subtleness of the French conciliation approach at Kissingen as tools for wrenching apart the entente and, using the Moroccan question as a cover for broader concerns, argued for the "Panther."

The perceptions of the Germans in late June showed little understanding of the French position. The French were finally willing to negotiate German compensation for French control of Morocco. It was for this reason that Cambon sought out Kiderlen at Killingen. There was no need to coerce the French at this point. And, the impact of the "Panther" on the French was precisely the opposite of that which the Germans had envisioned. The French were astounded by the unnecessary German coercion. They were uncertain of its meaning, but the general tenor of their speculation was pessimistic. The Germans, so the French thought, must be trying to take advantage of the French conciliatory approach expressed at Kissingen. Rather than accepting these gestures in good faith, they were trying to reap windfalls from the French willingness to compromise and to drive a harder bargain. The French suspected the move to be a response to Cambon's insistence that Morocco would not be ground for compensation (Caillaux, 1933: 14-51; Tabouis, 1938: 209). Thus they felt the "Panther" might be a demand for the intolerable—a partition of Morocco, and war would come before the French accepted this outcome. Even if this pessimistic interpretation proved to be an exaggeration, the French were reluctant to give anything at gunpoint which they might have parceled out through calm negotiation. The "Panther" increased the stakes of the current conflict through what knuckling under to its pressure might imply about future and ever more frequent Franco-German confrontations. And the French were angered by the crass and unnecessary act of gunboat diplomacy which could only be designed to humiliate them. These reactions bolstered the position of those French leaders who resisted dealing with the Germans.

Although some German publics, particularly powerful economic interests, were demanding their government gain control of southern Morocco, the German government at this stage was willing to settle for compensation elsewhere (Jaeckh, 1924: 129). The Germans had discussed partition with the French in the spring, and although they would have welcomed a partition, they were not demanding one. Their thoughts were turning toward the French Congo. So the "Panther" was a counterproductive signal in that its message about compensation was misunderstood and its method stiffened French resistance. In addition it was extraordinarily poorly timed (Schoen, 1922: 147-148). Caillaux, who followed Monis as premier, was as favorably disposed toward Franco-German rapprochement as any French leader. In his previous capacity as finance minister he had held unofficial discussions with German representatives in which a free French hand in Morocco in return for German compensation in the French Congo had been discussed. Now Caillaux, barely in office, found himself confronted with what appeared to the French to be a provocative German demand for partition. This discredited his conciliatory perspective from the very beginning and made Caillaux's domestic position precarious. And as their own conciliatory initiative appeared checked, the French deferred further action, sounded out their allies for support, and waited for a clearer statement of German intentions.

THE BRITISH DILEMMA

The perceived German hostility caused the French to look to their British allies for support. Their pleas found two schools of thought within the British foreign office (Nicolson, 1930: 240-241). One position was held by Nicolson and Crowe who saw a continental league looming behind almost every European, especially German, diplomatic action. They advocated staunch support of France in order to hold the Entente Cordiale together. With respect to the Moroccan question some British leaders of this persuasion were particularly sensitive to the possibility of a German naval base in the general area of Gibraltar and thus opposed any agreement which gave Germany Moroccan territory. Grey, the foreign secretary, advocated a more cautious policy. He too feared a continental league, but he was acutely aware that strong British support of the French against Germany could draw the British into a struggle with Germany over values almost exclusively French. Grey recognized what the French were trying to do in Morocco. He had considerable sympathy for the German desire for compensation, and he was reluctant to see Britain pay for aggrandizement of the French colonial empire in terms of increased German hostility. Thus when Grey met with Metternich, the German ambassador to London, on July 4th, he emphasized only that any freedom of action which the Germans had won through the new Moroccan situation could be exercised by the British as well. Grey was uncertain as to the meaning of the "Panther" and he stressed to Metternich the necessity for British concurrence in any new settlement of the Moroccan question. Having essentially marked time with respect to the Germans, Grey advised caution and urged continued conciliatory efforts on the French.

THE GERMAN SETTLEMENT OFFER

After some diplomatic hassling, Kiderlen and Jules Cambon began discussions in Berlin over the settlement of the dispute. Both men were bitter as the first meeting began on July 9th. Cambon was angered by what he viewed as a German breech of faith since the Kissingen meetings. Kiderlen complained that his experience with French good faith necessitated the precautions he had taken. The pace picked up rapidly after the initial recriminations, however. Somehow—each claimed the other initiated the subject—compensation in the French Congo was broached. Kiderlen approved of this and even offered a territorial exchange to ease the French ordeal. The progress of this meeting heartened all parties, but the discussions took a turn for the worse on July 15th when Kiderlen completed the "Panther's" signal by presenting the German compensation position in detail. Kiderlen wanted a large portion of the French Congo—including all the prize land such as the Atlantic coast and the Congo River frontage (Morel, 1918: 154). In return Kiderlen offered Togo and the northern part of the Cameroons in addition to a free hand for the French in Morocco. Cambon was astounded by the size of Kiderlen's demands. He refused the German offer on the spot. The French leadership interpreted Kiderlen's demands as too outrageous to be serious, and some suspected Kiderlen was trying to drive the negotiations back to a partition of Morocco by being totally unreasonable in his Congo position.

Kiderlen's actions were beginning to arouse concern not only among the French but with Kaiser Wilhelm and Chancellor Bethmann-Hollweg as well. The kaiser thought Kiderlen was creating a situation far more dangerous than merited by the prospective benefits. But for the time being Kiderlen overcame private domestic criticism of his actions and stuck to his position.[8] The French were inclined to rest on the strength of their position in Morocco and leave the next move up to the Germans. But Grey was exerting pressure for a compromise, and Cambon was told to make a more modest counterproposal (Documents diplomatiques français, 1955:

85-88). In addition to offering a concession proposal, the Quai d'Orsay leaked an edited version of the German position of July 15th to the French press and the British foreign office. The leak failed to mention the Germans were offering an exchange of territory and it concentrated on the German demand of the French Congo in return for a vague promise of French preeminence in Morocco—a promise which the French already had by virtue of the Franco-German accord of 1909. The distorted picture the British held of these negotiations helped to precipitate an event through which the Franco-German conflict was eclipsed by Anglo-German hostility.

THE MANSION HOUSE SPEECH

Since Grey's conversation with Metternich on July 4th, Paul Cambon (the French ambassador to London and brother of Jules Cambon in Berlin) had provided what the British knew about the atmosphere of the Franco-German talks by indicating to Nicolson on July 10 that the discussions were progressing along the lines of compensation in the Congo. Grey had been pleased with this approach. Now as French fears arose, the British too began to worry more about German intentions. Although Grey urged compromise initiatives on the French, his concern prompted him to speak again with Metternich on July 21st. Grey explained Britain was concerned about German intentions on the Moroccan question, but he did not demonstrate enough urgency to alarm Metternich and to cause him to warn his superiors something was amiss. Metternich only surmised the British felt a breakdown possible in the Kiderlen-Cambon talks and wanted to participate in whatever decision procedure followed them.

Grey's relative calm was not shared by Lloyd George, chancellor of the exchequer. Lloyd George was piqued that the Germans had not answered what he regarded as the British query of July 4th on German intentions. The Germans did not even realize a query had been made, and indeed the British statement of July 4th contained no query.[9] Yet it is clear that several British leaders felt the Germans owed them an explanation. On the afternoon of July 21st (after Grey's visit with Metternich) Lloyd George consulted with Asquith (the British prime minister) and Grey about the propriety of adding a bit on foreign policy to a speech he was to give before a London bankers' association that evening. Without making any specific references to the ongoing Franco-German crisis, Lloyd George stated that, although war was normally unthinkable in international affairs, there were humiliations worse than war. When nations sought to violate Britain's vital interests without consulting Britain, such humiliation developed. Gritain would follow the only course open in a predicament of this nature—war.[10]

The impact of the Mansion House speech was surprisingly severe since there was little in the speech which was revealing. But the Germans were surprised by the appearance of a threat at this juncture as well as by the method and the source. Kiderlen understood Britain would fight for its vital interests. But he felt the Germans had taken great care not to endanger such interests. Lloyd George's brusk statement to the contrary caught Kiderlen unawares. In any case the Germans would have expected an announcement of their failure to shield British interests to come through conventional, private diplomacy, not to appear in a humiliating public speech. And for Lloyd George to break the news was even more astonishing. Lloyd George was a sometime pacifist and was generally the member of the British cabinet most favorably disposed toward Germany. The British and then the continental press picked up Lloyd George's own vague wording and formed his speech into a belligerent threat. There was a period between July 22nd and 25th in which the British cabinet contemplated stating the speech was not an official cabinet position rather than passively accepting the most vigorous interpretations of the press, but this train of thought ended with Metternich's visit to Grey on July 25th (Asquith, 1930: 151).

Kiderlen had understandably interpreted Grey's conversation with Metternich on July 4th as a statement of the British position rather than as a query about the German stand, but it is a bit surprising that the unexpectedly tough policy followed by the French did not cause the Germans to reevaluate the analysis in their memoranda of May 3rd and June 12th. As Barlow (1940: 304) says: "Germany perhaps did not know that British temper was not inclined to tolerate further delay, but German success dictated that British temper should not be severely taxed." Yet Kiderlen was irate when he learned of the speech and particularly of its interpretations in the press. To his mind the Germans had been careful not to violate the British interests, but even if the British feared such an occurrence, the public threat of the Mansion House speech was unnecessarily demeaning. The obvious British response would have been an inquiry through normal, secret diplomacy. But, since the British had felt the necessity of humiliating Germany through public denunciation, Germany could and would play tough as well. The German response to the speech at Mansion House was thus quite similar to the French response to the "Panther" which the Germans had found so enigmatic. Kiderlen was reluctant to make any conciliatory gesture since such an effort might develop British images of a servile Germany which would give in whenever faced with firmness. And the speech simply made Kiderlen mad. While not exactly gunboat diplomacy of the nature of the "Panther," the Mansion House speech did circumvent normal diplomatic channels and create public humiliation. At this moment Kiderlen wanted revenge for his injured sense of propriety, not conciliation. Metternich divulged Kiderlen's anger to Grey on July 25th. Metternich closed this session with the warning that the more Germany was threatened, the more firmly the Germans would stand their ground (Lepsius et al., 1925: 213-214). These words caused Grey considerable anxiety, and he quickly went about London warning other government leaders that, from the words of the German ambassador, the British fleet might be attacked at any moment.[11] The interpretation of German intentions which Grey developed as a result of this exchange was that the Germans were trying to break the Entente Cordiale by humiliating France and were irritated with the British for intervening and ruining their plans (Lowe and Dockrill, 1972: 42).

CONTINUATION OF THE CRISIS

The week or so which followed Lloyd George's speech at Mansion House marked the zenith in the conflicting interests of the Agadir crisis. The French, still apprehensive about German intentions over Morocco, continued to chafe under the humiliation of the "Panther" and Kiderlen's —to the French mind—preposterous demands in the Congo. The Germans, already vexed by an unexpectedly stiff French resistance, now faced what they regarded as the totally unprovoked, wanton intervention of the British. And the British, in spite of Grey's efforts to restrain the French by exhibiting a noncommittal attitude and to restrain the Germans through a mildly critical stance, found themselves facing an intense conflict and bearing the brunt of German hostility.

The impact of the threatening French Moroccan coup, the "Panther" and the Mansion House speech sobered all parties somewhat and fostered efforts to draw back from the brink of impending disaster. In spite of this common inclination, the preceding threats had engaged additional values and developed righteous indignation which made withdrawal difficult. All three parties felt they were victims of malicious and in some cases whimsical manipulation on the part of their adversaries. They had great difficulty restraining themselves so as to resolve rather than exacerbate the crisis, and a number of minor incidents occurred before the tensions of the crisis began to relax in early September. A French endeavor to manipulate the Germans was the most interesting of these.

CAILLAUX'S EIGHT DAYS BLUFF

Caillaux represented the section of French leadership which favored rapprochement with Germany. He recognized that many French government officials—politicians and bureaucrats—despised his conciliatory orientation, and he desired to intervene personally in the Agadir affair so rapprochement would not be subverted by his countrymen. One of the early matters settled by Cambon and Kiderlen in their first post-"Panther" meeting on July 9th was a peculiar communications system through which certain sections of the sessions were reported directly to Caillaux rather than to de Selves at the Quai d'Orsay. This arrangement kept the more chauvinistic elements of French officialdom in the dark over particular aspects of the negotiations (Barlow, 1940: 258-260). In a further effort to check revanchist forces Caillaux initiated some independent negotiations between a personal representative and Schoen in Paris. These private negotiations were later publicized in the French senate investigations of Caillaux's handling of the Agadir crisis, and the public hearings led to cries of treason and the fall of the Caillaux government in January 1912. As an index of Caillaux's attitude on foreign affairs, the negotiations continued to serve as ammunition for Caillaux's enemies and contributed to Caillaux's being jailed several years later (Caillaux, 1920: 264).

Caillaux's representative at these negotiations, Fondère, met with Lancken-Wakenitz (the German emissary for Schoen and Kiderlen) on several occasions during the final days of July, and Caillaux offered terms through this medium which were considerably more generous than those being offered simultaneously by Cambon in Berlin (Lancken-Wakenitz, 1931). Caillaux desired a speedy solution to the conflict. He was also concerned that an agreement be reached during the August lull while both parliaments were out of session. If an agreement were completed during this lull, Cambon felt both he and Kiderlen would have a jump on their most rabid domestic opposition. Kiderlen, however, was still claiming to be willing to go to "extreme lengths" in order to achieve his suggestion of July 15th which was greater compensation than Caillaux was willing to offer even through this private forum, and these auxiliary negotiations lapsed for want of an agreement.

It is possible that Kiderlen's reluctance to reach an agreement at this time arose, not only from his manifest arguments about the necessity of significant compensation to safeguard Germany's European position, but also from latent desires to forestall a substantive agreement with France long enough to open a crack in the entente. If so Kiderlen grossly misperceived the positions of both the French and the British. Caillaux, even under threat of imminent war, could not have survived the concessions asked for by Kiderlen on July 15th. He would simply have been replaced by a hard-line premier had he accepted this solution. Continued German pressure of this nature was apt to lead to war. And, as the British perceived growing German pressure of France in late July, they moved to support the French more closely. The kaiser and the chancellor recognized the dangers of Kiderlen's policy and called him for a conference at the end of July. The content of their meetings was not recorded, but Kiderlen emerged from the sessions in early August more willing to compromise with the French.

Since the gap between the concessions the French were willing to grant and those which Kiderlen was demanding remained, by early August Caillaux in a fashion similar to Kiderlen before him felt that the response to his carrot might be more encouraging if it were stimulated by an example of his stick. On August 4th Fondère met with Schoen and declared, among other things, that if agreement over concessions were not reached within eight days, French and British warships would be sent to Agadir. The three nations shared a perception that a naval confrontation of this nature would be tantamount to a declaration of war. Nevertheless, Kiderlen's reaction to this threat was stern and swift. He instructed Schoen to have no further relations with the French government. Germany was not going to be pushed around at the whim of the French premier. Kaiser Willhelm was livid—virtually blind with rage—and he urged even more vigorous action on Kiderlen, and for once Kiderlen served as a restraining influence on his superiors. After a few hours' reflection Kiderlen relaxed his own stance, cancelled his previous message to Schoen, and instructed him to inform Fondère that, unless the threat was withdrawn, negotiations would be broken off. Caillaux stalled for several days, but Kiderlen had called his bluff. On August 8th he told Schoen he had been misquoted by his intermediary and he had never made a threat about naval intervention. The Germans grudgingly accepted this use of a loophole.

THE AGADIR SETTLEMENT AND AFTERMATH

A crisis atmosphere and dangerous occurrences continued for about another month after Caillaux's eight days bluff. Both Kiderlen and Caillaux were more anxious for a settlement than they dared appear for risk of difficulties or defeat respectively at the hands of more ardent nationalists (Grey, 1925: 223; Schoen, 1922: 151). But the two governments did not reach an accord on the dispute until November 4th. Discussions before their respective parliaments continued for several months thereafter. The substantive results of the crisis were that France gained its protectorate in Morocco—except for a Spanish fringe on the Mediterranean littoral—and received in addition a small piece of territory between the Chari and Logone rivers adjacent to the German Cameroons. Germany gained an enlargement of its Cameroons to the east and south. The enlargement, mostly swampland, included a short stretch of Atlantic coastline just south of Rio Mundi as well as a brief access strip to the Congo River which split the French Congo into two pieces (Morel, 1918: 154). The symbolic aftermath of the Agadir crisis dwarfed these substantive results. Images of hostility and feeling of fear and mistrust were heightened for the French and British with respect to the Germans; for the Germans with respect to the British; and, to a lesser degree, for the Germans with respect to the French. Agadir hardened the battlelines for the war which followed in 1914. And it contributed to the images which precipitated that conflict as its humiliations—particularly the "Panther" and the Mansion House speech—brought to prominence in France and Germany a group of leaders ringing the cry: "No more Agadir's!"

CONCLUSIONS

The Agadir crisis demonstrates threats, or at least vague perceptions of anticipated harm, can have productive results. The Germans felt they needed compensation in return for the French coup in Morocco. The French were initially reluctant to allow compensation, and it is doubtful whether the French would have spontaneously granted compensation in the complete absence of sanctions. The operative sanctions appear to have been British coolness toward exclusively French gains and a vague notion of German retribution. The specific German threat which materialized, the "Panther," was *not* the operative or even a productive threat. In addition, at a time when the Germans were pushing the French quite hard, the Mansion House speech awakened the Wilhelmstrasse to the possibility of British intervention and forced the Germans to come to grips with the dangers inherent in their existing strategy.

In spite of these contributions the various threats of the Agadir crisis were either unnecessary (the "Panther"), or unnecessarily severe either in the demands made (Caillaux's eight day bluff), or in the method of implementation (the Mansion House speech), and they shared two important drawbacks. They created grave risks in the immediate situation which could have easily resulted in war, and they left in their wake a lingering sense of hostility which fueled a devastating conflict in the future. So the Agadir crisis also indicates that the productive range of threat application is circumscribed and threats must be implemented with care if they are to be useful in managing and resolving conflicts of interest.

MISPERCEPTION PATTERNS

One set of difficulties which plagued the various national leadership groups involved in Agadir was the parochial nature of their national perspectives. The three sets of national leaders caught up in the crisis clashed on a limited set of conflicting issues which could have been calmly resolved at Kissingen. But the various national leaders held distorted perceptions which magnified the issues at stake and led through threats to escalated conflict activity. The Germans were persistent in their demands for compensation and harsh in their approach to the French because of their encirclement fears. Yet neither the French nor the British intended any offensive activity toward Germany. The French, and particularly segments of the British, were sensitive to German intransigence and bruskness since they perceived these aspects of German policy as indices of bold and far-reaching schemes for the expansion of German influence. Yet the Germans felt they were striving desperately to hold on to their existing European position and saw little opportunity for the luxury of expansion. The parties to the Agadir crisis tended to focus their attention on those signals of other nations which could be interpreted as hostile. Thus they developed exaggerated perceptions of the other's threats to their interests. This selective focus of attention stemmed partially from the long history of conflict over the Moroccan question which conditioned the diplomats involved to view this question in terms of threats.

Agadir's substantive payoffs, achieved at great immediate risk and long-term costs in deteriorated relations, were German recognition of the French position in Morocco—debased by the necessity of sharing this position with the Spanish and by German compensation which split the French Congo—and German control over a piece of marshland in west central Africa of such little use as to cause the resignation of the frustrated colonial minister, Lindequist. Several related misperceptions allowed this inequity between costs and benefits to develop. Each party exaggerated this error with an exalted notion of its own legitimacy. The statesmen of Agadir conceived of threats in terms of their own perceptions of anticipated harm and virtually ignored possibilities that the targets of their own influence efforts might feel threatened. Additionally, each party assumed its adversaries would back down in the face of firmness. These misperceptions resulted in relations virtually devoid of empathy or reciprocity. The leaders of each nation took firm stands with respect to the unprovoked aggression they perceived themselves to suffer at the adversary's hands, while often remaining oblivious to threatening aspects of their own policies and expecting the adversary to retreat as they asserted their legitimate rights.

The French, for instance, never recognized the entente or their effort to control Morocco as threatening to the Germans. What the French saw as a threat was wanton German intervention in an internationally recognized sphere of French influence where the Germans had no legitimate interests. The French were determined to rebuff this threat with a firm stand, even though the Germans did not perceive their desires for compensation as threatening to anyone. The Germans recognized the "Panther" as a threat to France—although they varied in recognizing it as an indirect threat to Britain, but they grievously misperceived the impact their threat would have on the entente powers. They supposed it would facilitate French compensation; whereas it blunted the ongoing French compensation initiative. And Kiderlen's hopes that the British would remain aloof from German pressure on the French were quashed by the Mansion House speech. The British varied in the speed with which they perceived the threatening character of the Mansion House speech, and certainly some—Grey, for instance—did not anticipate the sternness of Kiderlen's reply. While the threat achieved some success in this endeavor, the success was marred by the unforseen severity of the Angle-German hostility which the speech created. Caillaux knew he was threatening Kiderlen with his eight days statement, but he made an error about its impact similar to that which the Wilhelmstrasse had made about the "Panther." The Germans arose in fury over this provocation, and Caillaux was forced to back down before he could continue negotiations on the substantive issues at stake. The failure of these parties—both as threat initiators and as targets—to perceive that other parties might reasonably draw different conclusions abou the intentions prompting the various actions comprising the crisis, contributed to a conflict spiral which expanded the conflict latent in the pre-crisis situation. While conflicting interests were present and were revealed by the crisis activities, the threats used by the various parties created additional and largely unnecessary conflict issues.

Prudent threat policies simply demand greater recognition of the parochial bias and security dilemma fears inherent in various national perspectives. Statesmen should recognize that international signals are transmitted in an atmosphere of fear and suspicion to targets enormously sensitive to the most trivial negative interpretation and prone to build an image of resolve from each instance of conflict. The suggestion that national leaders exercise greater discrimination in estimating the impact of threats imposed on them by adversaries, and greater care in recognizing the nature and impact of the threats they direct toward others, appears ridiculously straightforward. Yet Agadir was hardly the initial instance of severe international misperception, and in the six decades since the crisis the mistakes of the French, German and British statesmen have been repeated regularly. Perceptual problems may indeed be more inexorable now than sixty years ago. The gulfs separating the conceptual worlds of Western, Soviet and Third World leaders today are surely deeper than the conceptual rifts between Grey, Kiderlen and Caillaux in 1911. The statesmen of Agadir, living near the end of the European international system, all shared many basic values and differed primarily on desires for a particular national preeminence.

It is difficult to imagine perspectives more thoroughly disparate than those of the current leaderships of the United States and North Vietnam. The Vietnamese leaders have little understanding as to how their nationalist movement threatens legitimate United States interests. Notions of imperialism which stress the necessity of war and control of raw materials for the maintenance of capitalist society may provide Vietnamese leaders with a rationale for United States involvement, but they would doubtless gape incredulously before Western perceptions of an international communist conspiracy, and they fight the imposition of harsh measures perceived as arising from efforts to sustain Western economies. The only way these men have of recognizing themselves as threats to United States interests so defies reciprocity and empathy as to be of negligible value in developing mutual understanding. And United States leaders have repeatedly supported what they view as their legitimate defensive intentions with the argument that, in contrast to the North, they do not want to conquer another part of Vietnam but only to secure the South. They seem incapable of regarding the contrived, Western oriented regime in the South as a threat to Vietnamese nationalism. Additionally, each national unit repeatedly misestimated the impact of escalation on the other. These miscalculations were criticized by strategists disassociated from the escalation policies of each side, and Chinese criticism of Vietnamese efforts to move prematurely to a conventional conflict (Lin Piao, 1967) has aspects which parallel Western criticism of the United States escalation policy. For several years the primary payoff of these miscalculations was increased costs for both sides. Bridging the tremendous differences in national experience between these two nations so as to reduce misperception is certainly a difficult task, but the costs of the last decade surely offer an incentive to try.

Yet in spite of the costs of misperception in Southeast Asia, some United States leaders continue to advocate preparing for the severest possibilities imaginable regardless of the likelihood of these contingencies. Such advocacy remains prominent today, in a context of growing European détente, as it was in Europe prior to the First World War. As pressures for relaxing the Soviet-American competition in strategic armaments have grown, military spokesmen have cited evidence which they interpret as indicating the Soviet Union is striving for a first strike capability (New York Times, 1969). And, as momentum grows behind plans for reducing United States forces in Western Europe, these forces, which few have seriously considered adequate to withstand an unlikely Soviet onslaught, are suddenly characterized by the military as meeting the criteria for flexible response and publicized as requisite for national security (Schmidt, 1973). While these statements are properly explained largely in terms of narrow bureaucratic perspectives striving to protect their vested interests, the arguments appeal to the familiar realist algorithm of preparing for the worst imaginable contingencies. Indeed the military seems more concerned with Soviet capabilities during an era of détente than it was during some periods of the cold war. It is perhaps understandable that the military should voice such fears. It would be discouraging if these opinions should be considered at face value in less parochial circles.

THREAT VULNERABILITY AND COMMITTAL THREATS

Another set of difficulties encountered by the actors in the Agadir crisis involved instances of particularly counterproductive threat impact. False estimates of the target's vulnerability to threats and the use—or the target's perception of the use—of committal threats, contributed to these counterproductive instances. Contrary to the false perceptions through which each party tended to exaggerate the threat vulnerability of its target, the three parties to the Agadir crisis were not highly vulnerable to threats. The long, crisis strewn Franco-German struggle over Morocco had slowly raised the stakes for both sides so that neither would back down completely without a fight although there was room for compromise. The French were willing to compensate the Germans, and the Germans were willing to accept compensation in a locality other than Morocco. But the French would have fought to avoid a partition of Morocco, and the Wilhelmstrasse was committed to achieving French acceptance of the principle of compensation and was probably capable of landing Germany in a war over this issue. As conflict over the Moroccan question developed in the Agadir crisis, such broad stakes were threatened that the British were drawn in through the Entente Cordiale. And the British position in 1911 was similar to the policy of 1914 which drew them into war once they were actually faced with the choice of aiding France in the struggle with Germany or witnessing a French defeat. The increased stakes and irritation resulting from the threats of the past had gradually reduced the threat vulnerability of the various parties so that intransigence on the part of any one might lead to war for all three.

Against this background of mistrust, apprehension and hostility the threatening actions entailing the Agadir crisis were particularly damaging. If the threats had been limited to warnings which delineated tolerance boundaries and, in the process of pointing out these necessary goals, clarified where room for compromise existed, the negative aspects of threats would have been reduced and possibly outweighed by positive contributions (George et al., 1971). In contrast to committal threats, warnings carry a reduced cargo of the drawbacks associated with threats. A warning informs an adversary of the mutual dangers entailed in violating an existing commitment and impresses on the target's mind the boundaries of crucial issues so the adversary can develop compromises which circumvent essential values. Committal threats build new, enlarged commitments in the context of an ongoing conflict. They exude arbitrary, even whimsical, flavor which emphasizes for the target the long-term consequences of allowing such a precedent to be set and may even irritate the target to the point that he is uable to respond with strategic action and resorts to fighting blindly instead. Misperception can play havoc with this distinction in that targets may erroneously perceive warnings as committal threats. Brusk coercive tactics and the sudden announcement of commitment positions for which inadequate groundwork has been laid contribute to misperception of this nature.

The threats of the Agadir crisis were not limited to a warning-clarification function or were not perceived as being so limited, and their counterproductive aspects predominated. Violations of the warning-clarification principle occurred in one, or both, of two ways. One violation was substantive. That is, a threat appeared to contribute to a new and unnecessarily grandiose commitment in terms of substantive issues. The other violation was procedural. Here threats violated diplomatic conventions in an unnecessarily blatant fashion, so that the method of the demands—rather than their substance—became the focal point of resistance. The particularly damaging aspect shared by both of these violations was an effort on the part of the threat initiator which exceeded (or was perceived by the target as exceeding) the defense of minimal tolerances and amounted to a search for whatever gratuitous windfalls the target could be coerced into conceding.

The threat of the French coup in Morocco which so disturbed the Germans engaged values and created anger through the method of implementation rather than through the substance of the threat. The Germans could have lived with a French Morocco. If France had not already set a precedent for payoffs with Italy, Britain and Spain, it is probable that the Germans would have been relatively unconcerned with compensation. But the precedent had been set, and from the German perspective their exclusion portended evil days for Germany's European position. The Germans could not perceive of this threat as a minimal French position or warning. To them their exclusion was contrived in the extreme and represented an unnecessary and deliberate affront to their position. The French method here virtually guaranteed German resistance. The Germans felt themselves victims of a whimsical French humiliation campaign. This angered the Germans and engaged additional values for them. If Germany did not draw the line here, it could expect to be pushed around with ever increasing frequency in the future (Gooch, 1938: 221).

French opinion of this activity presents an interesting contrast to German perceptions. The French could not accept the continual German efforts to barge into the Moroccan question as signals of German tolerances or warnings. To the French the German efforts were wanton aggression. The "Panther" was the height of German folly in this regard. In contrast to the impact of the French coup on the Germans (which was excessive only in method), the "Panther" struck an issue of grave substantive importance—as well as violating French sensibilities about proper diplomacy. Since the French had reluctantly come to accept the principle of German compensation and had said so at Kissingen, the "Panther" seemed to be directed at Cambon's insistence that compensation would not come from Morocco, and this perception raised the stakes enormously. The integrity of their Moroccan protectorate was important to the French, and the "Panther" offered an ominous lesson for the future as well. If the French did not resist German coercion in this blatant instance and teach the Germans the futility of this path, the future would devolve into ever more frequent displays of coercion. And instead of allowing the French to compensate at least under the appearance of their own initiative, the "Panther" placed the French in the humiliating position of knuckling under to a crass example of gunboat diplomacy. To the French the "Panther" was a typical German response to conciliation. Statesmen had to be tough with the Germans because the Germans repaid conciliation with humiliation. It rankled the French to have to deal with, much less compensate, men of such bad faith.

Lloyd George's speech at Mansion House violated methods of statecraft and not substance. The Germans, even Kiderlen and the others in the Wilhelmstrasse, were not eager to face France *and* Britain. But Kiderlen felt he had carefully designed German strategy so as to circumvent British interests. The "Panther" had anchored in a southern Moroccan port distant from Gibraltar and the Germans sought compensation far to the south in the French Congo. Unfortunately the Germans had neglected to keep the British well informed of their compensation position and had underestimated the impact they would have on the British through exerting pressure on the French. The British were uneasy as a result of these German miscalculations, and their response was the Mansion House speech. The Germans, aware only of their efforts to shield British interests and not of their blunders, simply could not perceive Lloyd George's speech as a mere warning. Even the possibility of British misperception failed to explain British activity for them. The Germans recognized the British could have misperceived German policy, but in this case the British warning would have come through conventional, secret diplomacy. Grey had tried this subtle approach, but Metternich failed to get the message, and the Germans could ascertain no other reason for the public speech than a British desire to humiliate them. This unnecessarily severe coercion angered the Wilhelmstrasse and engaged additional values through the precedent its passive acceptance might set. Kiderlen's response through Metternich was brusk enough to create a frenzy in London. German leaders less closely associated with Kiderlen's policy on the Moroccan question, Kaiser Wilhelm II and Chancellor Bethmann-Hollweg, were able to see the futility of Kiderlen's path and to draw Germany back from the brink of disaster in spite of the negative aspects of Lloyd George's speech.

Caillaux's eight days bluff is the clearest example of a committal threat in the Agadir crisis. Caillaux attempted to construct a commitment to an obviously peripheral state of affairs which gave the Germans the unmistakable impression of whimsical manipulation. Caillaux tried to move too swiftly from a mild mannered try-and-see approach, which had focused on his carrot, to an ultimatum. In building his coercive endeavor so swiftly he failed to convince the Germans that he was warning them of an existing commitment (cf. George et al., 1971: 232). Caillaux was unable to convince the Germans of any plausible reason as to why eight days was a crucial deadline; indeed there was no reason and the deadline was arbitrary. Such blatant coercion altered the orientation of several German leaders—most notable the kaiser—toward the conflict. These leaders were simply fed up with being pushed around by the French-British entente, and their reaction to Caillaux's latest humiliating tactic was practically hysterical. Kiderlen reacted with unusual restraint, but Caillaux's statement represented an unconscionable demand for him as well. If Kiderlen let Caillaux get away with an action of this nature, the future of German diplomacy would be terrible to contemplate, so Kiderlen called Caillaux's bluff.

The lessons of the Agadir crisis admonish statesmen to be content with delivering low-key warnings which delineate their existing tolerance boundaries and clarify the possibilities for compromise. Surely statesmen should steer clear of brinkmanship in the form of constructing new, broader and less credible commitments during a conflict or choosing particularly humiliating methods of stating their demands—since such threats may actually destroy the threat vulnerability of the target. The development of a new and broader commitment, particularly during a conflict episode, leaves the target with the impression that the initiator is striving to camouflage peripheral interests as core values. The target interprets such efforts as arbitrary and bespeaking designs for gratuitous gains, at the very least. Targets can also perceive threats of this variety as whimsical manipulative efforts. This perception characteristically develops anger, and anger often diminishes the target's grip on a strategic response.

Tactics which humiliate the target by method rather than substance can, through their seemingly unnecessary provocation, contribute to the target's perception of the initiator's arbitrariness. But a greater danger of humiliating a target through provocative acts lies in driving him from a deliberative mode of action to a gut response based on anger. Both the impression that the threat initiator is misrepresenting peripheral objectives as crucial interests and anger are apt to make a target less vulnerable to threats. A target's perception of arbitrariness on the part of a threat initiator creates in the target's mind the notion that the initiator can back down with little cost, and thus is apt to do so if the target stands firm. More importantly, targets are generally unwilling to allow their adversaries to succeed in building commitments of dubious salience due to the unpleasant precedence such acquiescence might set for potential future conflicts. Anger acts to reduce a target's vulnerability to threats by stripping away the realm of strategic action altogether. Misperception and points on which interests actually conflict are liable to create enough problems for warnings; anything more adventuresome carries a grave risk of being counterproductive.

In spite of much evidence of the counterproductive effects, the careless and virulent implementation of communicative threats and the use of committal threats persists into the contemporary period. In fact, a decade of cold war strategic theory has propounded the merits of brinkmanship (Schelling, 1960 and 1966; Kahn, 1961 and 1965; and Payne, 1970). Although much of this literature provides valuable considerations for the use of force in international affairs, it is generally written from an orientation which glorifies both a parochial United States—or occasionally another national—perspective and a cavalier attitude toward coercion. The nation the strategic theorist favors, invariably a nation which longs for peace and undertakes hostile actions only to defend itself from aggression, is confronted by expansionist adversaries which maintain constant pressure as they search for weakness in their target. Fortunately for the theorist's side, these adversaries (in spite of their aggressive tendencies) act in a cowardly fashion; when their probes are confronted with firmness, they back down. Their expansionist efforts stem largely from perceptions of weakness in the target, and their probes can be repulsed with the harshest methods without fear of retaliation since they represent the pursuit of peripheral aspirations rather than the defense of core values. Perspectives of this nature are usually mythical. In actual conflicts, legitimate defense of core values and wanton aggressive activity are rarely so conveniently allotted to opposing parties—and brusk coercive tactics will not always produce the success forseen by some contemporary strategic theorists.

The tendency for brusk committal threats to exacerbate conflict can be seen clearly in the activities of the terrorists in Northern Ireland and the Middle East. Committal threats are used in these conflicts primarily for the purpose of mobilizing greater segments of sympathetic populations to dissident action. In the short-run these tactics are not designed to resolve conflict and often have the impact—perhaps occasionally unintentional—of forestalling any resolution of conflicting interests which ignores the problems of the terrorist groups. Threats on the part of Irish terrorists to kill one member of the opposing constituency a day until their grievances have been redressed tend to reduce the threat vulnerability of opposing factions—including those charged with law and order. While such threats signal grievances in a manner which is difficult to ignore, the threats are peripheral to the concrete interests in conflict. The terrorists do not need a death a day; such an objective is only remotely—whimsically—related to actual grievances, and threats to impose deaths for peripheral objectives give rise to anger and hard-line stances on the part of opposing factions and would-be authorities. Of course, these stances serve the terrorists' purposes of radicalization. The terror in the Middle East creates similar reactions. Dead Israeli athletes in Munich (and threats of similar actions to come) signal frustration and grievance, but not productively from the standpoint of resolving conflict. These threats, too, are remote from the issues crucial to the initiating groups. The Palestinians do not need dead Israelis scattered around the globe; they need a viable homeland.[12] Terrorism fails to win this goal, but it has made a settlement of the conflict among Middle Eastern nations—a settlement apt to leave refugee aspirations unfulfilled—more difficult.

PROBLEMS WITH DOMESTIC POLITIES

Another set of difficulties, which reduced the efficacy of threats in the Agadir crisis, were the revanchist and other parochial attitudes of a variety of prominent domestic publics. The Agadir crisis represents a case in which the threat vulnerability of the formal foreign policy elites was greater than the vulnerability of other influential groups. Intra-national differences in threat vulnerability in this case were inversely associated with degrees of misperception over the breadth of values threatened by foreign adversaries and with self-interest in hard-line policies. For instance, some German businesses with concrete interests in Morocco perceived the French Moroccan protectorate as leading to the rape of Germany by hordes of black Moorish soldiers in the pay of France, and they vigorously opposed Kiderlen's willingness to accept compensation outside of Morocco. In cases of dramatic power imbalance—asymmetrical games such as Bully-Chicken—foreign threats may simply overwhelm the influence of domestic factors within the weaker nation. But these instances are rare, and statesmen normally face domestic pressures and threats as compelling as those thrust on them by foreign adversaries. For instances in which foreign and domestic threats are approximately balanced, warnings which indicate limits on the initiating nation's aspirations and offer possibilities for compromise are particularly useful in facilitating the diplomat's search for a solution which meets the demands of both the foreign adversary and the domestic polity.

Caillaux faced the severest pressure from chauvinist forces of any statesman in the Agadir case, and he paid for his rapprochement efforts through the fall of his cabinet and eventually a prison sentence. Costs such as these offer poignant examples of the folly a statesman can incur by taking lightly what powerful domestic interests deem threatening. Kiderlen was more fortunate than Caillaux in that, until the "eight days" episode, Kiderlen's superiors tried to hold him back. But Kiderlen too faced hard-line pressures. His colleagues in the Wilhelmstrasse were sources of hard-line advice, and colonial and business interests waged a vociferous campaign against what they considered his "no win" policy. What these groups wanted was the Sous valley of southern Morocco, and this concern was so popular in Germany that advertisements for the Pan-German pamphlet *West Morokko Deutsch* appeared in the socialist newspaper *Vorwaerts*. Grey—and his policy of restraint—was simply outmaneuvered by colleagues in the cabinet and foreign office who felt the German threat had to be handled more rigorously.

The international elite which directed foreign affairs in the European system prior to the First World War was probably more familiar with the operations of politics within the various member states than the national leaders of the contemporary global system. But unrecognized implications of the differences among the national units involved in the Agadir crisis also contributed to difficulties for the use of threats. Kiderlen for example was given surprising latitude by the kaiser, and as long as the kaiser was marginally satisfied with his performance, Kiderlen was relatively immune to other domestic pressures. In July, Kiderlen survived an unpublicized resignation attempt on the part of Lindequist (the colonial minister), who disagreed with Kiderlen's compensation proposals. A resignation of the French colonial minister, similar to Lindequist's successful autumn resignation in protest over the Moroccan accord, would almost surely have brought down the Caillaux cabinet. Caillaux held a weak position in contrast to Kiderlen—who had the strength to resist domestic threats and thus the strength to be tolerant with respect to foreign threats. The weak position of Caillaux's cabinet did not afford similar luxury. Had Kiderlen recognized Caillaux's predicament as Schoen (the German ambassador to Paris) did, he might have recognized the folly of the "Panther." He might then have sought a rapid compromise more arduously and thus have avoided the degree of French and British enmity which his protracted bruskness created.

Prudent statesmanship demands a threat initiator recognize that his target may well face domestic circumstances unfamiliar to the initiator, and the countervailing domestic forces with threats as powerful as the initiator's. Halperin and Kanter (1973) suggest that the difficulties a statesman faces on the domestic front have probably grown more severe than they were in the waning moments of the European international elite. Thompson (1972) certainly demonstrates severe difficulties in his chronology of the laborious domestic effort to counteract the hysteria of McCarthyism with respect to China. The growing ability of the United States to deal with China has developed, not through a change in the nature of the threat posed by China—a continually negligible factor, but through a change in the American polity. A decade's effort was necessary to obtain partial and grudging acceptance of the Chinese leadership as fellow members of the international system rather than as ruthless outlaws. Still, the fact that (after laying an intricate foundation) presidential leadership could be successful in changing the attitude of many sectors of American society—the mass media, for instance—is encouraging for the possibility of reducing the influence of the most chauvinistic elements of a society on international affairs.

A FINAL THOUGHT

From the viewpoint of peace research, the argument of this essay is both narrow and pessimistic. The argument that threats make positive, perhaps even essential, contributions to the resolution of international conflicts has been accepted, and no impetus has been provided for shifting international conflicts to more consensual modes of resolution. The acceptance of the central position of threats is admittedly sad and, while resting on a firm foundation of actual international conditions, lacks the creative idealism to open new frontiers in peace research. Instead the argument of this essay has sought to demonstrate that a variety of factors can, and regularly do, cause the use of threats to be counterproductive. From the standpoint of managing conflict activity so as to avoid mutually disastrous outcomes, there is room for improvement within threat oriented international interaction. Although this is a minimal argument addressed to self-interest, the cause of peace can be marginally served if threat initiators observe limitations on the efficacy of threats.

NOTES

1. Although the terms ally and adversary are used more appropriately to refer to tails of a continuous distribution than to describe discrete polar opposites, certain characteristics of the international system—the number of powers and the ideological heterogeneity, for instance—contribute to variations in the scope and flexibility of international relationships. In the bipolar, ideologically divided, cold war world, ally and adversary relations encompassed broad ranges of activity and were stable—while geographical limits or other criteria circumscribed the flexible alignments which typified the ideologically moderate periods of the European multipolar system.

2. Milburn (1973) focuses on a criterion similar to the distinction between warnings and committal threats. He argues that target compliance is closely linked to the target's perceptions of contingency. That is, if the target perceives application of the threatened sanctions to be contingent on his own action, he is more likely to comply with the threatener's demands. In order to gain target compliance then, Milburn suggests threats be coupled with limited demands which the target can reasonably accomplish. The notions of contingency (as used by Milburn) and limited

demands, are consistent with the warning concept developed in this essay. Further, Milburn suggests that large demands, which the target can meet only with great difficulty, destroy the target's perception of contingency and the likelihood of compliance. "If I feel that I shall barely succeed, if at all, in meeting another's demands, I may begin to suspect that his demands constitute a pseudocontingency, that the truth of the matter is he only seeks an excuse to inflict loss" (5-6). Pseudocontingency, like the committal threat concept introduced above, conjures the image of an adversary with aggressive, perhaps even whimsically, vindictive intentions. Compliance with threats of this nature offers little but humiliation in the present and a future plagued with new challenges.

3. While influential segments of domestic opinion often favor firmer stands with respect to foreign challenges than those preferred by foreign policy elites, this preference distribution does not always exist. For example, French public opinion in the Moroccan or Algeciras crisis of 1905-1906 was decidedly more soft-line than the policies of French foreign policy makers (Leaman, 1942).

4. This case study is abridged to emphasize limitations on the efficacy of threats. The standard account of the crisis is Barlow (1940).

5. Sontag (1933: 157) indicates a reluctance to initiate compromise proposals characterized the diplomacy of this period. Sontag offers no explanation as to why diplomats acted in this fashion, but Iklé's (1964) discussion of bargaining among nations clarifies this convention. The nation which makes specific proposals first reveals its expectations. In the absence of specific French proposals, the Germans might have asked for less than the French were willing to give. In this instance the French would have preserved values by remaining silent and responding to the German initiative. The Germans, realizing this weakness in initial proposals, might probe the French to make an initial suggestion which was more than they actually needed. The French for their part could rebut such a German suggestion with the argument that initial proposals are always exaggerations. This in fact was one attack which the French actually leveled at Kiderlen's subsequent offer of July 15th.

6. In all, three German ships were involved in Moroccan waters during the Agadir crisis. The "Panther" was joined by the cruiser "Berlin" and an additional gunboat, the "Eber." The precise movements of these ships were not discussed by the Germans during the crisis. Gooch and Temperley (1932: 846-847) give the general movements of the ships.

7. Wolff was editor of the *Berliner Tageblatt* from 1906 to 1933, and often a harsh critic of German foreign policy.

8. Kiderlen actually sent two resignations to Chancellor Bethmann-Hollweg after hearing the kaiser was less than pleased with his performance (Jaeckh, 1924: 128-130, 132-134). But the chancellor refused to accept either of these resignations.

9. Grey admits there was no explicit query of German intentions (Grey, 1925: 215).

10. There are differing interpretations of the Mansion House speech. Taylor (1954: 470) provides the maverick thesis that the speech was directed against the French. Cosgrove (1969: 698-701) provides a summary of the majority position, held (among others) by Lloyd George (1933: 40-42).

11. These warnings were taken seriously by some officials (Churchill, 1923: 47-48).

12. Some argue persuasively that *psychological* needs exist for Palestinian violence (Fanon, 1963) or for a homeland in familiar Palestine (Lerner, 1958). But

such needs are not conventionally recognized in diplomacy and are not apt to be persuasive in gaining concessions from the Israelis until the deprived groups have more power.

REFERENCES

ALLISON, G.T. and M. H. HALPERIN (1972) "Bureaucratic politics." World Politics 24 (Spring Supplement). 40-79.

ANDERSON, E. N. (1930) The First Moroccan Crisis. Chicago: Univ. of Chicago Press.

ANDREW, C. (1968) Théophile Delcassé and the Making of the Entente Cordiale. New York: Macmillan.

ASQUITH, H. H. (1930) The Genesis of the War. New York: Doran.

BALDWIN, D. A. (1971) "Thinking about threats." J. of Conflict Resolution 15 (March): 71-78.

BARLOW, I. C. (1940) The Agadir Crisis. Chapel Hill: Univ. of N. Carolina Press.

BARNET, R. J. (1968) Intervention and Revolution. New York: World.

BETHMANN-HOLLWEG, T. V. (1919) Betrachtungen zum Weltkriege. Volume 1. Berlin: Hobbing.

BROWN, R. G. (1970) Fashoda Reconsidered. Baltimore: Johns Hopkins Press.

CAILLAUX, J. (1933) D'Agadir à la grande pénitence. Paris: Flammarion.

——— (1920) Mes Prisons. 3rd ed. Paris: Editions de al Sirène.

CHURCHILL, W. S. (1923) The World Crisis. New York: Scribner's.

COSGROVE, R. A. (1969) "A note on Lloyd George's speech at Mansion House." Historical Journal 12 (No. 4): 698-701.

Current Digest of the Soviet Press (1963) "Khrushchev's speech at the German party congress—II." Volume 15 (February 20): 15-16.

Documents diplomatiques français: 1871-1914 (1955) 2nd Series, Volume 14. Paris: Imprimerie Nationale.

ELLSBERG, D. (1972) Papers on the War. New York: Simon & Schuster.

FANON, F. (1963) The Wretched of the Earth. (C. Farrington, translator) New York: Grove.

GEORGE, A. F., D. K. HALL and W. E. SIMONS (1971) The Limits of Coercive Diplomacy. Boston: Little, Brown. GOOCH, G. P. (1938) Before the War. Volume 2. London: Longmans.

——— and H. TEMPERLEY [eds.] (1932) British Documents on the Origins of the War: 1898-1914. Volume 7. London: H.M.S.O.

GREY, E. (1925) Twenty-Five Years: 1892-1916. Volume 1. New York: Stokes.

HALPERIN, M. H. and A. KANTER (1973) "The bureaucratic perspective," pp. 1-42 in M. H. Halperin and A. Kanter (eds.) Readings in American Foreign Policy. Boston: Little, Brown.

HERZ, J. H. (1951) Political Realism and Political Idealism. Chicago: Univ. of Chicago Press.

HILSMAN, R. (1964) To Move A Nation. New York: Dell.

JAECKH, E. [ed.] (1924) Kiderlen-Waechter. Volume 2. Stuttgart: Deutscher Verlag.

JERVIS, R. (forthcoming) Perception and International Relations.

——— (1968) "Hypotheses on misperception." World Politics 20 (April): 454-479.

KAHN, H. (1965) On Escalation. New York: Praeger.

——— (1961) On Thermonuclear War. Princeton: Princeton Univ. Press.

KENNEDY, R. F. (1969) Thirteen Days. New York: Norton.

IKLE, F. C. (1964) How Nations Negotiate. New York: Harper & Row.

LANCKEN-WAKENITZ, O. V. (1931) Meine Dreissig Dienstjahre. Berlin: Verlag fuer Kulturpolitik.

LEAMAN, B. R. (1942) "The influence of domestic policy on foreign affairs in France." J. of Modern History 14 (December): 449-479.

LEPSIUS, J., A. M. BARTHOLDY and F. THIMME [eds.] (1925) Die Grosse Politik der Europaeischen Kabinette: 1871-1914. Volume 29. Berlin: Deutsche Verlagsgesellschaft fuer Politik and Geschichte.

LERNER, D. (1958) The Passing of Traditional Society. New York: Free Press.

LIN PIAO (1967) Long Live the Victory of the People's War. Peking: Foreign Languages Press.

LLOYD GEORGE, D. (1933) War Memoirs: 1914-1915. Volume 1. Boston: Little, Brown.

LOWE, C. J. and M. L. DOCKRILL (1972) The Mirage of Power. Volume 1. London and Boston: Routledge.

MILBURN, T. W. (1973) "When do threats provoke violent responses?" Paper presented at the Int. Studies Assn. Convention, New York City, March 14-17.

MOREL, E. D. (1918) Ten Years of Secret Diplomacy. 6th ed. Manchester: National Labour Press.

NEUSTADT, R. E. (1970) Alliance Politics. New York: Columbia Univ. Press.

New York Times (1969) "Fulbright says Laird uses fear to promote ABM." (March 22): 1, 16.

NICOLSON, H. (1930) Portrait of a Diplomatist. Boston: Houghton Mifflin.

PAYNE, J. L. (1970) The American Threat. Chicago: Markham.

PICK, F. N. (1937) "New light on Agadir." Contemporary Rev. 152 (September): 325-333.

POINCARE, R. (1922) The Origins of the War. London: Cassell.

RAPOPORT, A. (1960) Fights, Games and Debates. Ann Arbor: Univ. of Michigan Press.

——— (1957) "Lewis Richardson's mathematical theory of war." J. of Conflict Resolution 1 (September): 249-299.

SCHELLING, T. C. (1966) Arms and Influence. New Haven: Yale Univ. Press.

——— (1960) The Strategy of Conflict. New York: Oxford Univ. Press.

SCHMIDT, D. A. (1973) "NATO can defend itself." Christian Science Monitor (July 18): 14.

SCHOEN, W. E. (1922) The Memoirs of an Ambassador. (C. Vesey, translator) London: Allen & Unwin.

SIGAL, L. V. (1970) "The 'rational policy' model and the Formosa straits crisis." Intl. Studies Q. 14 (June): 121-156.

SNYDER, G. H. (1971) "Prisoner's Dilemma' and 'Chicken' models in international politics." Intl. Studies Q. 15 (March): 66-103.

——— (1969) "Notes on threats, commitments and 'moves,' " Working Paper No. 2, Crisis Bargaining Project, Center for Intl. Conflict Studies, SUNY-Buffalo. (Mimeo)

SONTAG, R. J. (1933) European Diplomatic History: 1817-1932. New York: Century.

STOVER, B. (1971) "The Lebanese crisis." Crisis Bargaining Project, Center for Intl. Conflict Studies, SUNY-Buffalo. (Mimeo)

TABOUIS, G. (1938) The Life of Jules Cambon. (C. F. Atkinson, translator) London: Cape.

TAYLOR, A.J.P. (1954) The Struggle for Mastery in Europe: 1848:1918. Oxford: Oxford Univ. Press.

THOMPSON, J. C., Jr. (1972) "On the making of U.S. China policy, 1961-1969." China Q. 50 (April-June): 220-243.

VAGTS, A. (1956) Defense and Diplomacy. New York: Columbia Univ. Press.

WHITE R. K. (1966) "Misperception and the Vietnam war." J. of Social Issues 22 (July): 1-164.

WOLFF, T. (1936) The Eve of 1914. (E. W. Dickes, translator) New York: Knopf.

CHARLES LOCKHART received his Ph.D. in political science from the State University of New York at Buffalo in 1971. His primary interests lie in peace research focusing on the management and resolution of international conflicts. He is temporarily in military service.

A Better Way of Getting New Information

Research, survey and policy studies that say what needs to be said—no more, no less.

The Sage Papers Program

Five regularly-issued original paperback series that bring, at an unusually low cost, the timely writings and findings of the international scholarly community. Since the material is updated on a continuing basis, each series rapidly becomes a unique repository of vital information.

Authoritative, and frequently seminal, works that NEED to be available

- To scholars and practitioners
- In university and institutional libraries
- In departmental collections
- For classroom adoption

Sage Professional Papers

COMPARATIVE POLITICS SERIES
INTERNATIONAL STUDIES SERIES
ADMINISTRATIVE AND POLICY STUDIES SERIES
AMERICAN POLITICS SERIES

Sage Policy Papers

THE WASHINGTON PAPERS

SAGE PUBLICATIONS
The Publishers of Professional Social Science
Beverly Hills • London

Editors: **Harry Eckstein,** *Princeton University,* **Ted Robert Gurr,** *Northwestern University,* and **Aristide R. Zolberg,** *University of Chicago.*